Growing up female

Growing
up
female

a personal
photojournal

by Abigail
Heyman

Holt, Rinehart and Winston

New York   Chicago   San Francisco

Published simultaneously in Canada by Holt, Rinehart
and Winston of Canada, Limited.

Printed in the United States of America.

First Edition

Printed by Rapoport Printing Corp.

Library of Congress Cataloging in Publication Data

Heyman, Abigail, 1942–
    Growing up female.

    1. Women in the United States — Pictorial works.
I. Title.
HQ1426.H46   301.41'2'0973   73-16242
ISBN (Hardbound): 0-03-012451-4
ISBN (Paperback): 0-03-088387-3

For encouragement, counsel, and understanding that were essential to this book and to myself, I especially thank Charles Harbutt, Ken Heyman, Lee Jones, and Joan Liftin.

Designed by Arnold Skolnick

This book is about women, and their lives as women, from one feminist's point of view. It is about what women are doing, and what they are feeling, and how they are relating to their mates, their children, their friends, their work, their interests, and themselves.

This book is about myself. I looked at people and events long before I owned a camera, more as a silent observer than a participant, sensing this was a woman's place. It is no longer my place as a woman, but it remains my style as a photographer.

I have been a girl child and, in my expectations, a mother. I have tried to be prettier than I am. I have been treated as a sex object, and at times I have encouraged that. I have been married and have seen my husband's work as more important than my own, his decisions sounder than my own. And I have been divorced. I have been a premedical student and did not go on to medical school because I could not take my education seriously just as no one around me would. And so, instead, I have been a salesgirl, and a receptionist, and a full-time housewife. I have thought housewives and mothers did nothing of importance. I have disrespected all women but the rare woman who did what men did. I have disregarded women, as I disregarded myself. And I have changed. I have faced the conflicts inherent in growing up female, as I am now facing the conflicts in trying to change. This is where I come from; this is what I want to document.

These photographs include poor and middle-class and wealthy women, white and Black and Indian women, professional and literate and uneducated women. The problems and the strengths that women share come out of the experience of being a woman and cross all other sociological and class barriers.

I have photographed the problems and

strengths of women. Some have suggested that I photograph the solutions. I don't know the solutions. There are photographs of a lawyer and a doctor. There are photographs of a women's gynecological self-help demonstration and of a legal abortion. These solutions are significant, yet they are a small part of the book just as they are a small part of what must change. It is not that women must become lawyers and doctors and earn money and do "men's work." Rather, it is my hope that we will come to respect our own work and ourselves, be we doctors or nurses or mothers. We must come to respect "women's work" and women's qualities whether they are the same as men's or different.

This book is "a" feminist way of looking at women, but not "the" feminist way. People constantly ask me, "What do the feminists think of . . . ?" I can only answer for myself.

The short, personal excerpts from my diary have become my own. But they did not all originate with me. They came not from the women I photographed, but from the revelations and the questioning of myself, my friends, and members of consciousness-raising groups.

In these groups all of us have shared so much of our growing up and have supported so much of each other's continued growth that we have become sisters. It is often in these groups that I have heard, "*you feel* like that? My God, I thought only I felt like that!"

Consciousness-raising has literally meant to raise the consciousness of women as women — to bring to conscious awareness so many things we do and feel and take for granted as women. Only when we are aware of these, rather than what we imagine we should be doing and feeling, can we decide what we want to keep and what we want to change. We are discovering, individually, what being female does mean, and might mean. We are still growing.

My aunt used to say, "You're a pretty girl. You'll do well."

Being pretty was important. If you were ugly, no one asked you out. I was already a good athlete and smart. I had enough problems.

If I went out with a man who liked bowling, I liked bowling. If I went out with a man who was interested in string quartets, I was interested in string quartets. If a man asked me to go to a murder mystery movie, I loved murder mystery movies. It just didn't matter to me, if I liked to be with him. I was very adaptable.

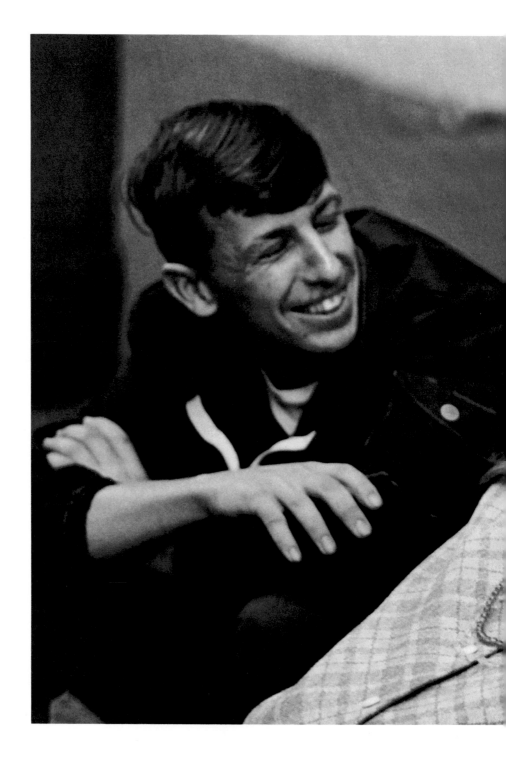

I am so conditioned

not to fight.

In a women's gynecological self-help group, I got to know my body — and myself — better. Have you ever looked at your cervix?

I have loved three men in my life.

The first time I didn't love myself. And he didn't love himself. We understood each other very well.

The second time I needed someone more secure than me. And he needed someone less secure than him. That was fine until I became more secure.

The third time I needed work as well as love and children and a home. He needed the same, and he wanted a full-time wife. That wasn't the only work I needed.

I have watched other mating relationships in the past few years. In these I have seen women who disliked themselves and lived with men who couldn't love. I have seen other women encouraged in their insecurity by their mates. I have seen other women giving up essential parts of themselves — their work, or their friends, or their interests — to be the primary force of emotional support and responsibility in a marriage-home-family that they had expected to share equally. I have seen abused women, and smothered women, and dependent women. Many are happily smothered or happily dependent. I have seen many successful mating relationships, in which each member prospered because of the relationship — but none that I could identify as a relationship I want.

As I have seen more women taking control of their lives and considering themselves important, becoming fuller, more whole people, valuing themselves and becoming more independent and assertive, I have seen the breakup of mating relationships. I'm not sure that has to be so. But I'm not sure that it doesn't.

In spite of what I've experienced and observed, I still cling to the image of a relationship between a man and a woman in which each can function better,

and grow further, and love more because
of the other. Sometimes all this has
seemed so close that I still believe
it's possible.

But always, as those relationships

became more intimate, I felt instead
how they limited my growth, how the
compromises required to keep the
relationship alive were deadening important
parts of me, and I decided that my
wholeness was more important than the
love. But I miss that kind of love
a lot.

And still I wonder what's so
radically wrong with me, so absolutely
unlovable about me, that no man has
ever loved me in a way that I can now
respect as love.

How then do I want to love again?
How then do I want to be loved? I only

know I don't want to be loved in the irresponsible way that I could only respect when I didn't love myself. Or in the possessive way that seemed right when I saw myself as a dependent person. Or in the adoring way that I could eagerly accept only when that love was the only thing I wanted in life.

"You don't marry the man, you marry the life."

My grandmother told me, "There is
a man 95 years old and he wants to
marry me. He wants a woman to take
care of him. Men have a lot to gain by
marriage. I'm 85 and I need a wife too."

At first I didn't want my husband
in the delivery room because I didn't want
him to see me that exposed. And I was
afraid he would never want to make love
with me again.

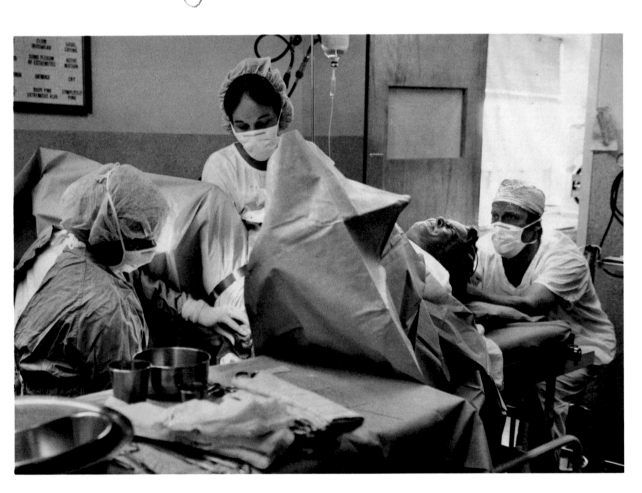

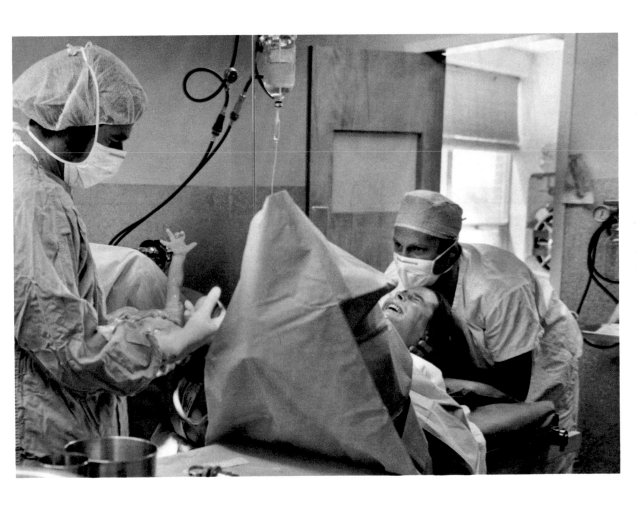

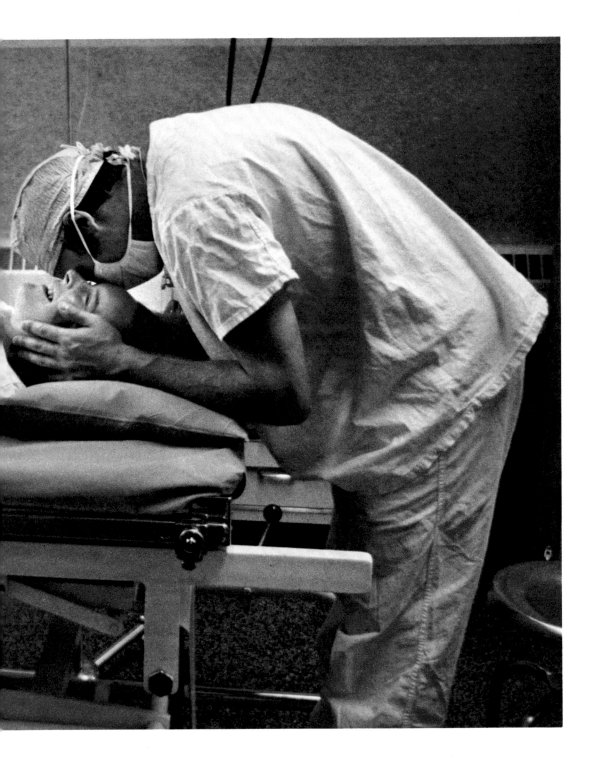

Nothing ever made me feel more like a sex object than

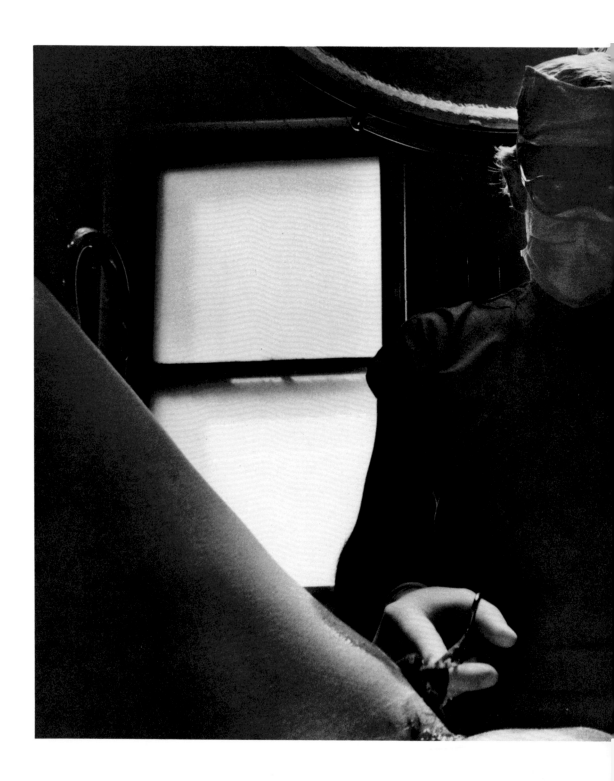

going through an abortion alone.

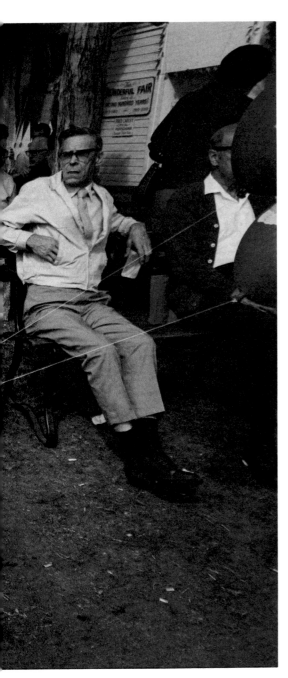

When I was a little girl I thought
that playing with dolls was stupid and that
playing games like the boys did was really
exciting. Later I thought I liked
man-conversation better, that girl-talk
was stupid. Now it seems to me that
girls were talking about real things like
dolls and babies and love. We've been
denying that the really important talk is
important. We've been putting ourselves down.

I have very clear ideas about what a man should be and I've tried to teach my son that, but the reason I didn't want a daughter was I didn't know what I wanted to teach her about being a woman.

I've told him he can be strong. He should be strong, and he should be smart. I don't know if she should be strong. I don't know if that's the right thing to tell her or not. Men tell me, "You're so strong." I think with my husband if I hadn't been so God damn strong, he would have been stronger.

I am no longer flattered when men tell me I don't think like a woman.

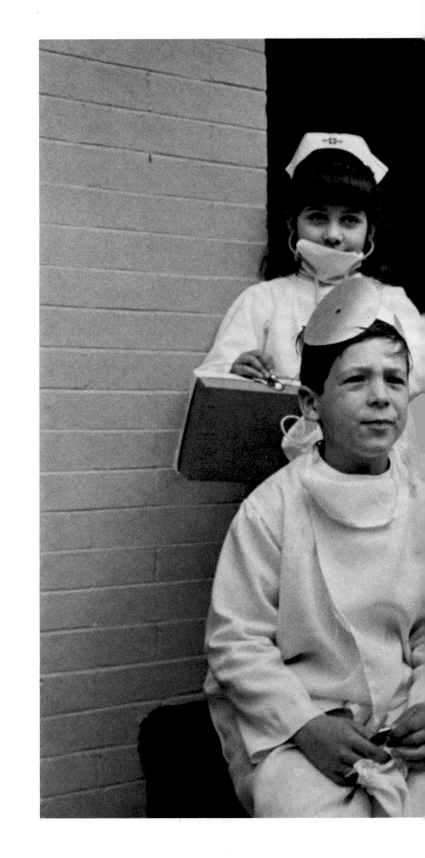

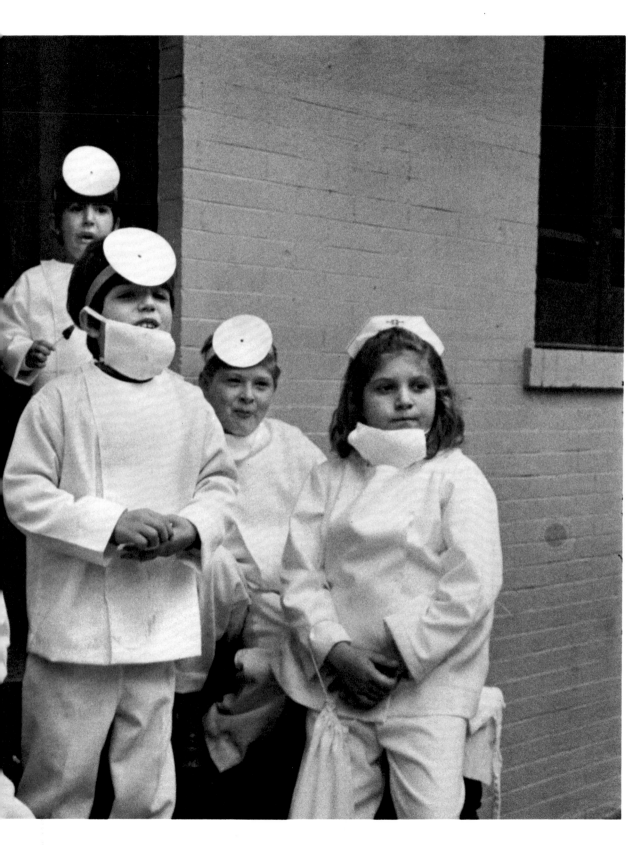

The question is not whether women should work. Of course we work. The real question for many is whether men will take equal responsibility in raising children so that we are not the only partner holding two jobs.

Dave and I do share the housework.
Sometimes that scares me. If he doesn't

need me for that, I'm afraid maybe soon
he won't need me at all.

I'm not sure how many of the things I do are natural for women and how many are culturally imposed. I'm not sure what to just accept and what to question. Having to question every mode of behavior and every expectation that I've grown up with is the best part and the scariest part of being a woman today.

I don't feel guilty anymore that I hate doing dishes and stuff like that, and I've gotten rid of feeling that I'm crazy because I'm not content with what I'm supposed to be content with. I'm doing things I wanted to do before but I wasn't sure if wanting them was right.

Now I'm not afraid of being bright, or of not being beautiful, or of having an ego of my own. I'm not afraid to be assertive, or to take control of my life, or to consider myself important. I value women. I value myself. I don't reject being female anymore. I can become the woman I want to be, and I can help to develop a new society that will value her.